D1047432

POEMS SIX

BOOKS BY ALAN DUGAN

Poems
Poems 2
Poems 3
Collected Poems
Poems 4
New and Collected Poems: 1961–1983
(includes *Poems 5*)
Poems 6

Alan Dugan
POEMS SIX

THE ECCO PRESS
New York

The Ecco Press
26 West 17th Street
New York, NY 10011

Published simultaneously in Canada by
Penguin Books Canada Ltd., Ontario
Printed in the United States of America
Designed by Design Oasis
FIRST EDITION

Grateful acknowledgment is made to the editors of the following periodicals in which some of the poems in this collection originally appeared: *The American Poetry Review, Poetry, Provincetown Arts Magazine, Ploughshares,* and *Antaeus.*

Library of Congress Cataloging-in-Publication Data
Dugan, Alan.
[Selections. 1989]
Poems 6/Alan Dugan.—1st ed.
p. cm.—(American poetry series)
I. Title. II. Title: Poems six. III. Series.
PS3554.U33A6 1989 811'.54—dc19 88-34701

ISBN 0-88001-199-8 (cloth)
ISBN 0-88001-225-0 (paper)

The text of this book is set in
Sabon Antiqua.

For Judy

CONTENTS

TAKEOFF ON ARMAGEDDON

—for Ronald Reagan

As we tour the field in the pause
before the final battle, you can see
the flowers growing upside down
among the opposing troops. The roses
look like hairy turds in the dirt
and the insects are behaving like animals
gone wild in the stench because God rots.
They have stung everybody involved:
the forces of good and the forces of evil
are stuck: it's them against them,
they're exactly equal, exactly the same,
there's nothing to fight about, it's all over,
they have all been fundamentally stung.
They stand there forever, paralyzed in shit.
They wanted Armageddon, they got it.
This concludes the tour of the battlefield.

As we move beyond good and evil let us hope
a sexy hunger for catastrophe does not revive them
from their statuesque military postures because
the final battle will be, you know, the final battle,
and then there will be no more good, no more evil,
no more beyond good and no more beyond evil,
no more roses growing upside down in the dirt,
no more insects, and no more you and your rotten God.

ON FLOWERS. ON NEGATIVE EVOLUTION

When the front-end loader ran over my wife's Montauk daisies
I wanted to tell the driver, Butch—a nice kid—but couldn't:
"No flowers, no us. Flowers are basic to human life.
That's why we think they're beautiful. No flowers, no seeds;
no seeds, no greenery; no greenery, no oxygen: we
couldn't even breathe without them. Also: no greens,
no grasses; no grasses, no herbivorous animals;
no animals, no beefsteaks. There wouldn't be anything
to eat except fish, and no way to breathe unless
we went back to the ocean and redeveloped gills.
There the seaweeds would make oxygen by flowering underwater,
the way it used to be in the old days, and you
would be running over them in your submarine. This is why
flowers are thought beautiful, and this is why it's important
not to destroy too many of them carelessly, and why you could
have been more careful with my wife's god-damned daisies."

ON NAMING A BABY MIMOSA

Oh sensitive mimosa, you have
more feelings than most other plants
because you shrink up at my touch
but no more brains, so why
should I say anything to you? Because:
you remind me of that touchy blond
baby I love and hate, who does not
listen to me either. Therefore I say:
Go bloom your pretty flowers while,
wherever, and as much as you can,
because I'm tired of talking here alone:
I feel like the devil and god mixed up as a man,
and if you do not listen to me,
and you can not listen to me (no ears),
and if you do not look out for me,
and you can not look out for me (no eyes),
I am going to bomb your whole
dirty world out from under you
and blow your radioactivated seed
out to the stars above your dumb heads,
but you, you will not understand,
because you have (again) no brains,
or know that sunburned baby's name:
Abounding in Likeness; otiose; mime.

SURVIVING THE HURRICANE

When the neighbor's outhouse went by
and landed upside down on my property,
unoccupied, I laughed and yelled, "It's mine,"
but what's so funny? the TV says
that many, many will get blown away
in the hurricane's uproarious humors,
and now the horizontal rain comes through
my wall, the wallpaper heaves and cries
and runs down to the floor as pulp
as the windows go out with the wind,
poof!, and the wind picks off the roof
two shingles at a time in love-me-nots,
and there is no difference inside or out:
Leaning against the wall or the wind
is the same. This wet is that wet.
There is no protection anywhere except
I go stand in the upside-down outhouse
with the crapper over my stinking head,
once it has dripped dry of its storm-borne shit,
and be the dry mummy of its sarcophagus
under the whole hurricane of the universe.
That's what's so funny: Egypt.

AN ENVY OF NATURAL FORMAL LIBERTIES

You birds stay out all night
in all the weathers all the time.
Oh how I envy you
and the departure of your
beauties from the coming cold.
First five, then seven more,
that makes twelve, a flock,
uncountable in process of migration,
maybe a hundred birds go up and down the air,
working a globe, a rough one,
changing all the time in time
in various transparencies
to hit the ground without
a bounce, there's nothing:—
I couldn't see them in the grass
unless I knew that they were there.

Then they're up again. They're
black birds screaming all as one
except for a few gone strays,
and line up on the wires between the poles
in flight from spheres to flats to lines,
in flight from three to two dimensions,
from four to three to two in time:

they are so still at rest
it is all one.

Two weeks to Labor Day, you
flying fools!, the stronger first,
the weaker later in a V: That's
the natural formation flying
life to death for you! Then
you're off to Florida for the winter
in that permanent vacation of the free
you're always working at for all your lives.
Oh may I too work my passage free
and make the Key West to my desiring
when my great Labor Day arrives.

CODA

You birds don't work for strangers
because you have no hands:
you just happen to be free.
What about those other birds
who have to work their beaks,
clap wings, and dance their feet,
cooped up in cages so some boss
will throw them grit to eat?
If nobody clipped their wings,
why don't they beak the lock,

claw down the door, take off,
and head for the horizon where
your flying answers freely are.

MEMORIES OF A BOSS IN AN AD AGENCY

He walked around dictating
what could be his profit
in his necessity, jingling
the balls of his coins
in his pants pockets. He
was money and money talks.
He talked and was the one
whose talk we sickened at.
Nausea was his atmosphere.
Open an office door
at his shop and Aargh!,
panic appeared: we froze.
That was his sex: he
told me when I quit:
"Power is what I want
the way you want to be
a whore. You think
you'll stop getting screwed
just because you're leaving here.
No way. You're made for it."
He laughed until he coughed
the come of his life up
and spat it in my ear.
I gave birth to this
economically maladjusted poem.

LOVE AND MONEY

The United States of America is like a convention
    of the International Baton Twirlers Association
in Johnstown, Pennsylvania, during a steelworkers' strike
    when I went there once as a bill collector.
The locked-out mill-workers on the street corners
    stared at the nearly bare-assed middle-class girls
dressed in nothing but expensive glittery rags
    with a dirty gray lust for money and cunt,
but they didn't touch the girls or the mills
    because they weren't theirs. Right and wrong.
The girls weren't theirs but the mills were theirs
    because they built them, ran them, and made
everything in them except the money: it went away
    to where the girls were, so they stood around
without the money and watched the girls.
    Therefore I took the money and flew
back to New York to tell the liberal conservatives
    that the republican democrats are right:
There is no left-wing politics in America left.
    There is the International Baton Twirlers Association.

MARXIST ANALYSIS OF THE FIFTH LABOR OF HERCULES

The Augean stables were so full of horseshit
that the Augean nobles came to laugh at Hercules
when he was told to muck them out by hand.
They hoped to see him filthy on his knees,
all asshole and elbows going fast for years.
Instead he wrenched a river from its bed upstream
and set wild water roaring through the place
and washed it all away, all
the horseshit, and I mean all
the horseshit, —the horseshit, the horses,
the stables, and the nobles too,
standing around ready to bugger Him,
Hercules, Wrestler of Rivers. Conclusion:
Revolting conditions elicit revolutionary solutions.

MEMORIES OF THE BOWERY

"pray for me and die rotten," the men's-
room wall read. "I don't want a drink,"
the old whore said. "You know what I
want. Come on. Come on. Come on."
"You couldn't come if you was asked,"
the bartender said, so she walked out
screaming into the traffic but the truck
stopped: she couldn't even get run over.
"God protects them," several people said.
How the air smells best on leaving a bar
broke in the morning with nothing to do
but be at present at Liberty's harbor
under the protection of that goddess,
and sit in Battery Park and feed
my beer-nuts to her pigeons. Impossible.
The Juggernaut would never stop for me,
the way it would for the holy drunks,
so I went a few blocks north to join
the godforsaken whores in slavery.

REMEMBERING AN ACCOUNT EXECUTIVE

He had a back office in his older brother's
    advertising agency and understood the human asshole.
He turned his father's small inheritance over and over
    on hemorrhoid ads between three-hour lunches
at the Plaza every day and cocktails at five-thirty
    with different dressy women waiting in our front office.
We joked that he fucked them up the ass to make more customers
    and were nauseated by him because he picked his ears
with the lead end of his lead pencil as he argued and argued
    hemorrhoid copy with us on nauseating Mad. Ave. mornings.
Why argue? It must have been for executive power-feelings
    because the copy never changed. Every week, the poor
bleeding assholes bought the shit. When my mind
    began to get fucked and go as black as his inner ears
I quit as broke as I began, remembering his prophecy:
    that the last working television set in the world
would be showing a hemorrhoid ad for ANUSALL
    at Armageddon, that it would have been written
by him, that he would be watching it at 6:00 P.M.
    in the bomb-cellar lounge of the Park Plaza Hotel
with a blonde's ass in one hand and a scotch in the other,
    and that he would die happy, with his old man's
money intact and his asshole too, unlike us prat-boys.

MONOLOGUE FOR A SIXTH AVENUE SCREAMER

You don't know anything about city life.
Sometimes you were lucky to get out alive
from some of the places I used to go to,
and if you were lucky enough to get out alive
you were lucky you weren't killed outside the door
and if you weren't killed outside the door
you were lucky you weren't killed on the street
and if you weren't killed on the street
you were lucky you weren't killed in your apartment
because you know who you'd find in your apartment,
you you you, screaming in your toilet bowl:
            You God-damned shit.
            You God-damned turd.
      I hate the standard of your life.
      I hate the standard of your soul.

SEXIST LAMENT: RUIN BY MONITOR

When you came in the office saying "Hi
Honey, so this is where you work,"
my boss, my boss's bosses and the boss himself
stared out at me like Easter Island statues
from the television in the bugged room,
and when the bullhorn's word came down:
"Dugan, you should have kept your love outside,"
I knew I'd blown it and was in for hell.
Oh I got processed out into the gutter, ruined
with you. Good business is for gangsters organized
in fear, love, and doesn't let some girl
come kissingly to the money-works on payday.
They think that you're for lunch;
that you get bought and sold at night,
or that you're there to decorate the lobby.

EMPIRICAL SCENE

We saw a grand piano fall off a roof
as if in slow motion, and hit
the sidewalk without a sound
as we laughed at the philosophical implications
and went down into the subway
where the noise of all crashing pianos
is kept on permanent performance
at full volume, so at least we weren't deaf
or in an inconsistent universe.
It had been like the beginning of a silent movie
but we didn't know that we were in it
so we never found out what happened,
we, who didn't hear the grand piano.

ON PLUMBING AFTER AN AIR RAID

The houses have dropped their bricks
behind a screen of bomb dust
and become red rubble, fast,
where trees of plumbing stand
and bear their porcelain fruits—
sinks, bathtubs, toilet bowls—
four floors high in the air.
Oh let our hydraulic culture rise
new from our lead-pipe garbage heap
and geyser out of the fire storm
to fall back on our sewerage,
so that all lovers underground
may join their waters to the waters of life,
and the nude in the fourth-floor bathtub,
dead but sexy, and wholly exposed,
be the goddess of the city's fountain.

ON FINGERNAILS IN BLOODY TIMES

God help the fingernails:
they are cursed by atrophy
and are no longer claws,
just clarified visors glued
to tender quicks. What
nonsense that the fingers wear
shell born from the sea
and not more serious weapons.
Oh you can bite them, paint them,
scratch with them, or else
wonder why they are, by God,
but that's about it, right?
Wrong. Why do our torturers
rip them off so much?
Because they are the backups
for our grasp of things,
not just our caresses,
and are the delicate armor
over such a sensitivity
that we wouldn't even have the hands
comfortably to fight with
if we didn't have them on.
That's why they rip them off,
the pretty little fingernails.

ON A POCKETKNIFE. ON CARRYING

If only a maniac possessed it, he
could hone it on his thumb: it
could practice on a diet of split hairs
so as to flash across the flesh I fear
and make a night of ambulances and the police,
but now the rust of my neglect comes over it
like the disease of unrequited lovers in the old
romances. What catastrophes it makes me dream
of as it sharpens pencils near my skin:
Oh I can let it wander in the flesh of fruit,
but no slit throats, no hearts searched for
through the ribs, no outrage at the penis,
though sometimes I am so ashamed to waste
that passion keening from my pants' back pocket
for a course of blood, that I dream blood,
and walk at night knife-handed and afraid
to find the forehead of an innocent to sign.

Then if I anti-skate my thumb along its edge
my thumb weeps, and if it's pointed to my back
my back weeps, and if it's pointed at my front
it fills my stomach with the sweet ache
of an ugly prophecy I want to shit away
just when my cock and balls attempt to shrink
back to the safety that the running guts deny.

My face dares it. It wants the scar.
I see it flashing. I could lose my eyes.

The blade is junk except for what
it carries on its edge: the edge,
and what it carries on its point:
the point: that's where it narrows down
and vanishes: its point
and death for those it hits
is balanced on that fine frontier
between the gross shining metal
and nothing at all. That's where it's at.

TRAVEL ADVISORY FOR A NIGHT SHIFT

It is the kind of raw and changeable afternoon
when the undersides of the clouds are dark
but white on top because of the crazy weather
and the wind rolls beer cans in the gutters.
They're worth money but nobody picks them up.

The violence of the street people seems to give way
to that of the weather: they keep it all indoors,
apparently, and only the roaming New Jersey marks
in heated cars seem out for normal trouble and
the few poor street whores frozen naked to the ass.

Let those who can be warm inside be warm inside
while we, dear, get to go out dressed for a wild night.
We have to get from here to there by morning, which
is where the profit lies, and spend the night between
in making it between some pretty cold betweens.
So, let's watch it with that crazy weather in the street.

DEDICATION FOR A BUILDING

The excavation for the new
clinic of Bellevue Hospital
was littered with knocked bricks,
corrupt plaster, and old ward-
flowers thrown to the blasting-dust.
A cat grinned with the effort
as it chewed a piece of meat
fastened to a kraft paper bag
while some man slept off something.
May the new clinic rise to cure
all ills its site is host to,
and not mistreat the desperate.

OXYMORONIC HOSPITAL BLUES

I knew it was going to end badly
when you put the bouquet in my urinal.
When my nurses' aide saw it, she
yelled: "No good! Urinal for pee!
Need clean clean for test, Mr. Dopey!"
She said "Not again." I said "Never again,"
and she went to the sickroom john to clean it
while talking dirtily to three absent presences
named "Madre de Diós," "Diós Mío," and just "Madre."
She was a beautiful, small woman
to have such an ugly, large vocabulary,
so please do not contaminate
my piss-bottle with your flowers again:
it is just a classy gag
that overworks the underpaid.

Hold ID... HUN 5175
Hold Until: 07/09/15

PIK Hold Slip
Poems six.

BOAST

I've walked every walkable bridge
into and out of Manhattan and climbed
the towers of Brooklyn Bridge twice
and gotten the grease of the Roeblings' cables
all over my hands, face, and raincoat,
drunk illegally up there where the cables
groan on their supporting high rollers
            Hurray
and now I'm crippled in Manhattan, played out.

Should I have done a Brody
when I had the high body
rather than lie here in a flat?
No. Rather I celebrate the rain-
storm over the East River that night
that kept the police indoors
and lit the bridge with burning water
back to Brooklyn where I was born.

SOLILOQUY: GHOST DANCE FOR A CRIPPLE

Something has happened to the air: a fly
fiddled some of its hind legs together on
the white tablecloth, turned around three times,
and then turned over on its back and died.
This happened before World War Three
when everything is happening all over
and everything can be blown away.
Regardless of what Mao Tse-Tung says,
"The wild bear cannot frighten a brave man.
Even the plum tree is pleased with snow
and doesn't care about freezing or dying
    houseflies,"
I am afraid of the wild American animals
and am going to rip the white tablecloth off
the table and dress in it and catch
the dead fly as it flies through the dead air
and dance around this dead room
on my cane and good hip and bad hip,
wearing the tablecloth and with the dead fly
in my arms, in my mouth. I
am going to make fun of the whole process
because it's awful, and this is my ghost dance,
and it's all for you, but I am not
doing it: I'm a cripple: you're doing it.

PROVINCETOWN *TOTENTANZ*

(dance of the dead)

It's obscene, the way you have a girl's voice
and flirtatious manner in a broken-down old body.
When we stand together on canes at cocktail parties
you say, Let's kiss, nobody kisses anymore,
come on, kiss me, I'll give you AIDS.
Remembering how you felt when you were fifty,
I could get a hard-on if I could get a hard-on
so I send you off to get another zombie.
Then we can dance together later, drunk,
six-legged, bones to bones, we'll knock 'em dead,
you, the ancient flapper, me, who looks like death,
as figures in the comic strip The Plague Years
for these kids who never knew what it was like to kiss
everybody at the party!, regardless of the sex.

IN MEMORIAM: AURELIUS BATTAGLIA, AND AGAINST HIS TRAGIC SENSE OF LIFE

Aurelius Battaglia, the greatest loudmouth in the world,
has bored everybody to death and shouted down
everybody everywhere at cocktail parties and bars
in New York, Hollywood, London, Paris, Rome.
Now, when I meet him at Ciro's bar, he can't talk,
he's had an operation for cancer of the larynx,
he can only whisper, constantly, spitting in my ear:
he claims it's his fate, his destiny, his comeuppance,
he's being punished for the sin of hubris, of overweening pride,
he's paying out to all the people he has pissed off
by his immoral shouting domination of all conversation,
he feels proud of his own personal, ironic, and tragic fate
as the greatest loudmouth ever made silent by overuse
of his vocal cords resulting in absolutely just throat cancer.
I try to say, "Aurie, Aurie," although he cannot hear me
through his crazy whispering speculative egotistical logorrhea,
"Listen, Aurie, it's true that you have an appropriate fate,
that you're an offensive loudmouth shut up by throat cancer,
but don't really believe in appropriate fates or tragedies
or just punishments for hubris: that's just bullshit:
it might help you in your merely personal agony

but remember contingency, remember automobile
        accidents,
remember the random deaths of innocent people in wars,
politics, fires, epidemics, plane crashes, you name it,
we live like herds of animals, impersonal personal accidents
happen regardless of personal characteristics, vices or
        virtues.
So listen, Aurie, when you and I walk out of Ciro's drunk
        tonight
after the bars close, when we are still arguing this problem,
when you are not listening to me and I am not listening
        to you,
we could both get hit by one of the drunk drivers
        around here
and that would not be tragic, it wouldn't even be fate:
it would just be ridiculous: death. So, *Pace,* Aurie, *Pace.*"

ON THE DEATH OF NORMAN DUKES

When the poet was dying of cancer
he had to get rid of his airplane.
He couldn't fly anymore
and couldn't keep up with the payments:
it would be a burden on Nellie,
so he had to get rid of his airplane,
he wrote it over and over
in the last month of his journal:
he knew he was dying of cancer,
he couldn't fly anymore,
he couldn't keep up with the payments,
so he had to get rid of his airplane,
he wrote it over and over:
after a note against suicide
it was his last journal entry.

LAMENT FOR CELLISTS AND JACQUELINE DUPRÉ

When the beautiful cellist Jacqueline DuPré
died of multiple sclerosis at forty-two
all the cellists grieved, and one
fell on her instrument, not
as a sacrifice, but as an accident,
if there are such accidents. She was
hysterical, but there was no
damage to the tone, and it only cost
a thousand bucks to fix. Remember,
a cello is a beautiful shape of air
set in the right box and played by strings
played by strings the player plays:
the player can't get close to it the way
a violinist does, feeling the air play
the wood play the bones of his/her head
as the violinist joins the music to the brain.
That's why some cellists dance
with it like Yo Yo Ma, because it is
an outside music that they have to join
as athletes of a different air,
so when Jacqueline DuPré died young,
her muscles dying on her first,
it got to the cellists in their very art
because they're distant from their instrument:
it can't go to their heads, like violins.

With her, the music started distantly, then
it got more distant, then the distance
got to be the infinity of cello death
the way a cellist I knew would drape his tux
around his instrument before he went to sleep
after a performance in a strange town
so the cello could be the cellist through the night,
dead silent, with a black bow tie around its neck,
and he could joke away the horrors.

ON A BENIGN BUREAUCRATIZATION OF DEATH

After my father died fighting at
my mother for life as usual,
like the yard dog with the house cat,
I thought that she would sit and hide
for months like a damaged animal,
staring and mute until she saw
his shadow moving on the wall
from some car's headlights outside,
and start to screech at his ghost
for years in the empty house
like so many old Irish ladies do
until she got put away, too,

but she went to her sister's place
next to the funeral home upstate
that her sister's husband bought,
and aged out gossipy and sweet
about the quiet, prettified stiffs
she helped to dress next door,
because she knew the mortuary talk
was all business at the dinner table,
all rational, all accountable,
and she could get a good night's sleep.

STORY FOR ACTORS

There's a story that a traveling Greek actor
came to a Spanish town in Hellenistic times
to give a reading from Old Greek Tragedy,
but that when he went on in the amphitheater,
dressed in the horrible mask, the long robe,
and the high-soled star-actor's cothurni,
and roared out the terrible old lines
the poor hicks panicked, and some of them
got trampled to death in the stampede.
The municipal authorities were so stupid
that they banned Old Greek Tragedy forever
and executed the actor for mass murder.
That they killed him for being too great
is the greatest praise an actor could ever want,
but that they couldn't even write up his name
is proof of their own illiterate shittiness
and of his immortal anonymous fame.

ON A TRAVEL STORY FROM WORMWOOD VALLEY

When French monks stole the bones
of St. Benedict and his sister
St. Scholastica out of Italy
and smuggled them into France,
they split them up because
when holy thieves fall out
there's the devil to pay,
so one set went to Le Mans
and one to St. Benoît-sur-Loire,
but they say they got the sets mixed up,
so that there are two incomplete
brothers and sisters together
in holy partial skeletal incest forever or
until they join our general incest of dust or fire
in the flying coffin of this world.

ON A DESOLATION OF THE ANIMALS AT NIGHT

I used to think that the animals
were exempt from human suffering
because they had no brains, but now
I'm not so sure because I hear
two cats moaning on the windowsill,
sleeping in a desolation not to be denied.
Why is it that the dirt made flesh
must suffer for its intuitions for a while
before it goes back to its nature? Ha,
dancy cats? Ha, sleepers? Why
are the insides of your bone heads cleverer
than opals, onyx, and Egyptian goddesses?,
in bearing witness to what's what:
those roaring horrors of the universe,
the stars, if we could only hear them
burning outside the window while you cats
sleep moaning on the windowsill as I
watch out from something wondering inside.

NOTE

This is what your cat does
while you're at work this morning:
It sits in the middle of the room
and looks at something on the ceiling.
Then it gets up, stretches and smells
the chair legs and my legs
as I drink the coffee you
so kindly left me, silently.
Then it sits in the middle of the room again
and stares up at the ceiling again.
Then it gets up again and walks
around your apartment again
smelling legs in the silence: It's
driving me crazy. When I've left,
after locking the self-locking door
exactly as you told me to, dear,
I don't think the cat will notice
my absence the way I hope you will,
you cat-person, you cat-torturer, you
member of the Spay-Neuter Humane Society,
but will be staring up at something on
or through the ceiling all day long
and smelling out the paralyzed legs
of the locked-in chairs until tonight
when you come home and bring it food,
your moving legs, and your electric presence.

WHY THERE IS NO CLASS SOLIDARITY IN AMERICA I READ IT IN *THE TIMES.* AUG. 2, 1987

An Italian in Hackensack got mad
at the Jewish lady downstairs
and hired a Polish man with three rattlesnakes
to slip them under her door and kill her,
but her cats raised such an uproar
that the cops came and caught the snakes,
the Pole, and then the Italian
because the Pole ratted on the Italian
but who ratted on the Pole? The rattlesnakes?
One of the rattlesnakes bit one of the cats
but the cat recovered. All this proves
that there is no class solidarity in America,
and that cats are better than rattlesnakes
if they come from Hackensack and are Jewish cats.

SUBURBAN EXORCISM

When the witches' coven across the street
hung a dead rat from a pine-tree branch
across our access road, it was not for us,
it was an imitation of the crucifixion of Christ
done as a Black Mass for psychotherapy.
The witch-mother had a radio talk show
in Boston and explained it: God's rat
embodied the collective unconscious guilt
of her therapeutic community which got
exorcised as a dirty thing for mental health.
When my wife went to Town Hall to complain,
all the women in the office went Yuck,
and promised immediate action but the town
road gang wouldn't touch that stinking rat.
They took our whole god-damned pine tree out
with a front-end loader and burnt it,
so watch it: America is full of believers,
Black-Massers, witch-mothers and rat-hangers.

AMERICAN TOURIST TO A GUATEMALAN TARANTULA

You are the black prince of bananas,
so if I vandalize your yellow
upside-down Indian palace you have
the right to violence, but if
you trespass as the hairy crack
of chaos on my hotel bedroom wall,
here I am the lord, charged
with the place and lady, so
expect some breaking furniture, shouts,
and murder dancing in my shoes.
We exploit bananas. I stamp on you.

ON A SKUNKED FOX

I found out where the smell was coming from
when I looked under the beach-plum bush
and saw the skunked eyes of a fox looking at me.
He didn't even try to run off, as if to say,

"You are one of those killer human beings I
am supposed to run away from. Here I am.
Put me out of my misery," but I didn't do it,

so he walked away slowly and sat on a hilltop
as a target, scratching his eyes with the sides of his paws,
but nobody shot him, so he walked off again,
as if looking for a road to get run over on.

CARLA IS A HORSE LOVER

Carla bought an old horse
to save it from the glue factory.
She fed it, combed it,
and rode it carefully,
but it threw her. Then it
sat on her and broke her pelvis.
Now she can't take care of it
because she lost her job
because she's in the hospital,
and people say Carla!
Sell that horse to the glue factory!
but Carla says No!
My girlfriend Simpson
will take care of it,
and Simpson does.

THE DYING SEAGULL AND THE GREAT WHORE OF THE WORLD

The seagull sitting on the town beach must
have had a broken wing or foot: It didn't move,
with all the swimmers looking at it, when
a little girl dressed just like a child whore
in a red spangled bikini bottom and unnecessary bra
squatted down to pat it on the head.
It must have been waiting, in whole composure, for
the night's predators or the tide to take it out
to the death begun by natural breakage and
the minimal tourist attrition of the child's hand.

ON FISHING BEING A CHANCY LIFE

In Memoriam: John "Picky" Thomas

Once my wife and I were invited out trap-fishing because
the fishermen believed that tourists and women brought good luck.
When we climbed into the boat, a half-decked one, at dawn,
there was a gull trapped in the bilge, screaming. "Don't touch
that fucker," the captain, John Thomas, said. "She could
bite your fucking finger off." He grabbed the bird
by its shoulders and threw it up in the air.
The bird hung there into the wind, still screaming,
then started circling around the boat with the other gulls
so as to take part in the morning's fishing.
I was astonished by Thomas's pounding activity:
he must have weighed two hundred and thirty pounds
and had hands bigger than my feet, but
he moved with absolute delicacy and speed
in the rocking boat to throw the bird in the air
under the mottoes: "Don't hurt yourself." "Take care."
and, "A man can't be too careful of himself around here."

TOURISTIC NOTE FROM THE GULF

As the fishermen pulled up the giant manta ray
she gave live birth, and a dozen of her young
flopped back into the Gulf of México off Yucatán
where Mayan queens would pierce their tongues
with the ray's stingers, and the kings their pricks,
to keep the universe fertile and in proper operation, but
tonight the giant triangular wing-flaps
would go to every Chinese restaurant in town
for some of the identical reasons in soup:
as nourishment, laxative, and aphrodisiac.
That's what happens: the bloody old transcendence
winds up in cheap soup in a broken-down town,
and what can save the baby manta rays
from the destruction of the Gulf of México, ha?

CRITICISM OF BERGSON AND DARWIN

The primeval fish was like a squid, all mouth,
with eyes, ears, feelers, nostrils (or gills),
and ten tentacles set closely all around it.
The tentacles kept pushing food into the mouth.
The mouth was always snapping open and closed
with teeth: choppers in front, fangs at the sides,
grinders in back. Inside the mouth
a tongue was always lashing ground-up fish
and chopped-up seaweed into a rear gut.
Behind the gut there were two thrashing tails,
and between them there were two holes and a barb.
Fish bones and mash came out of one hole. The squid
put the barb into the other hole of another squid
while the other squid put its barb into
the other hole of the first squid. After a while
squid eggs came out of both of these holes,
and some of them floated ashore and became us.
What a tragedy. You lost your barb
and kept your hole. I lost my hole
and kept my barb. You get to make the babies.
Why? Why? Bergson and Darwin do not say.
Is this Creative Evolution? No. Is this
Origin of Species and Descent of Man? Yes.

SPEECH TO THE STUDENT CLOWNS AT THE CIRCUS CLOWN SCHOOL AT SARASOTA, FLORIDA

You innocents who want to play the clown
should be wounded combat veterans first.
You have to get the gut feeling, how,
when the fallen gladiator with a face
white in shock with two red spots
of panic on his cheekbones and his eyes
animal with black grief got the sign
thumbs down from the Emperor,
a bloody clown stripped off his face,
put it on, and danced around the ring
with a slapstick sword to tickle the crowd
as the corpse was dragged off by the heels.
This went on for centuries, centuries,
until you took up the mask and made it sad
or, worse, giggled, and made it sweet.
What happened? When serious art dies
in its wisdom, in American innocence,
even the bloody old farce of death dies.
Art must be ugly or lovely or both
to be beautiful, but not nice, terrible
in its pitiful humors, but not cute.
Ask the nasty children about this
some night before they're put to sleep
to clown around with the fiends.

ON HALLOWEEN

—after Kallimachos

The gorilla mask got put away
because we got too old
to see the face outside the face
inside, but it becomes
a Dionysius of Tragedy again
when a nephew puts it on
with the scary beast costume
and growls, "my hair is holy,"
"*telling me my own dream.*"

INTRODUCTION TO THE TELEPHONE

The telephone rang in the grocery store
and the grocery man said Answer it.
I was six years old and did. I said
Hello to the black mouth on the wall
and the black ear screamed in my ear.
I dropped it scared as he laughed
and I lost my telephone virginity
to the black howling universe of wire
looping out the plate-glass window, down
the Brooklyn avenue to New York City:
there, a vampire self of words sucks
money from that wire world, but I
am sick because it bit me in the ear.
I am adult to the instrument
and listen to the women angels' voices
calling the cities by their given names.

ELEGY FOR A MAGICIAN

Once I got so skinny
that I turned pale blue
in places and became ethereal
against the hard knocks
of the broken furniture
in the depression years,
but when my mother screamed
at me through one ear
to come and eat my beans,
the other ear stayed fixed
to the dying radio while
Chandu the Magician hissed
and whispered me away
inside his crackling box,
up the aerial and out
into the open airways as
the blue genie of Brooklyn.

MEMORIES OF 1936-7

When I walked my nazi girlfriend
home from public school I tight-
rope walked the curbstones while she
kept to the center of the sidewalk.
Although we didn't say a word she knew I loved her
blond braids and dirndl dress.
They kept a photograph of Hitler
on the mantelpiece between two candles,
and when he called the Volk in
they went: my first love sailed to the fire,
but not before her brother beat me up
unfairly: he kicked me in the balls.
I decided to kill Hitler, and did,
with the help of millions of others
like the Jewish kids on the block
who played "Burning Hitler's House"
with cardboard boxes in the gutter.
We were premature anti-Fascists
and my Dresden doll went to our fire early.

ON THE LONG ISLAND RAILROAD SYSTEM

I used to hate to ride the Long Island Railroad trains
to Rockaway Beach on Sunday mornings with my father
when I was an adolescent. He'd make me fake it that
my I myself was under twelve and half a fare when I was
        six feet tall
and fourteen. I didn't understand, in my grown rage
at being kept a child in knickers, not long pants,
that he was broke and showing me his own youth's way
out of his dry land life in Brooklyn and dead Queens
to the possibilities of the sometimes wild Atlantic Ocean,
pointing as a one-time sailor to the East, that there
was something going on out over there beyond the surf
and crowds of human bodies, girls!, playing in it,
that might be serious, dangerous, and worth it.

AUTOBIOGRAPHICAL LIBATION TO ERATO MUSE OF LYRIC POETRY

The baby-sized but skinny bronze statuette in a bronze
 Grecian robe
looks at a bronze butterfly on her raised bronze stink-finger
while the bronze lyre at her bare bronze toes lies unplucked
above the circular lead base where the anonymous hack sculptor
has caused to be inscribed ERATO MUSE OF LYRIC POETRY.
She's tarnished by bad air or else patinaed artificially,
oh my silence, and stood for all my boyhood on a pedestal
beside an unplayed grand piano in our unused lace-curtain
 living room.
I'd grab her by the neck and ankles when I got her alone
and pump her up and down as if she were a dumbbell
to get some muscle, while a sunbeam turned the room's
dust particles into star-ways possibly out of there
and the silence of the instruments: the piano, me, and her lyre.
I made a way out loud, unlike the piano and the statuette.
They stand there forever dead silent in the dead silent living room
where nothing moves except the sunbeam and the dust in the
 sunbeam.
The lace curtains might move, but only in their own wind
or in the solar wind, because the windows to the avenue are
 nailed shut
to the traffic leaving Brooklyn for New York and the Wild West.

SPEECH FOR AUDEN

You were out when I called.
The bottles under the sink
are proof of ecstasy enough
to show that you are working
but divorced again. Why
litter the floor with phrases?
"Spiritual mushrooms" I thought
quite good; the rest, interesting.
You American poets die
of alcohol, America, and lies;
of self-parody, bad sex,
Academia, and crankiness,
so do try to be pure
in your functional insanity,
and lock your door:
remember me.

RETRACTION

I gave up Art because
Art is lewd (Chaucer),
Art is immoral (Tolstoy),
and Art is useless (Rimbaud),
and went off slaving in
the Ethiopia of the Id
to buy my soul.
Ah what lewd immoral
useless things I did
to you, sweet love, before
you bit my hip off.

Now I've hobbled back
to where the battlements
of Wall Street rise
to sell my True Confessions
in the name of Christ,
transfigured into pure prosthesis
as the carrion bird
that Yeats saw on a coin
and advertised as golden.

FEBRUARY TWELFTH BIRTHDAY STATEMENT

That nameless son of a bitch of a critic who
wrote that I only wrote one good poem in
my life might be right so here's to you
future brother and sister and other poets
to drink to me and you with a shot
of bourbon and a bottle of beer
to the success of my intention on
my sixty-fifth birthday and to your
matching accomplishment. One poem
is enough. What have you two done,
my birthday mates Abraham Lincoln
and Tadeusz-Thaddeus Kościuszko,
to get a Lincoln Memorial and a Kos-
iosko Street in Brooklyn? Nothing
but revolutionary activity. That son
of a bitch of a critic has said it: I have
made one poem, not the Gettysburg Address,
and not the military fortifications at West Point.

POEM

After your first poetry reading
I shook hands with you
and got a hard-on. Thank you.
We know that old trees
can not feel a thing
when the green tips burst
through the tough bark in spring,
but that's the way it felt,
that's the Objective Correlative
between us poets, love:
a wholly unexpected pain
of something new breaking out
with something old about it
like your new radical poems,
those audible objects of love
breaking out through nerves
as you sweated up on stage,
going raw into painful air
for everyone to know.

SPRING SONG FOR *SYMPLOCARPUS FŒTIDA* AND ME

Any plant that makes its own spring
is the plant for me: that's why I am for
the skunk cabbage in the New Jersey swamps.
Its hot frost-thawing fart-gas
makes a hole in the snow late in February
and it comes up like a purple prick
with a hairy brown foreskin around
its base in the slush, and does it stink.
It's a great thing to see and smell on a raw day:
you can tell yourself: maybe I can make it too
for another spring, if this lousy stinkweed can do it.

ANSWER TO THE RILKE QUESTION

Wer, wenn ich schriee, hörte mich denn aus der *Engel*
Ordnungen?
Who, if I cried, would hear me out of the *Angel*
Orders?

Nobody. Berryman was right.[1]
You *were* a jerk. There *are*
no *Angels*. Especially Kraut
angels dressed up in Nazi
uniforms giving wing Heils.
They'd have to get *Ordnungs*
to answer your jerky cries,
so it's lucky you didn't cry,
but just said "*if* I cried,"
and used your life on great poems
like *Sonnets to Orpheus* who
didn't exist either, but so what?
Berryman was wrong, really.
You weren't really a jerk.
Berryman was really a jerk
to say a thing like that.

[1] See Berryman's *Dream Song 3*,
line 13: "Rilke was a *jerk*."

PRETRIAL HEARING

I thought she was a liberated woman
until I helped her in her kitchen
for our Faculty-Trustee Brunch.
Her big supply-side husband
kept on throwing sweeties,
honeys, darling baby dears
at her like bad old-fashioned
feather-boas which she didn't
want to wear but couldn't,
politely, duck, so she just
shrugged her shoulders as she
fiddled with the cocktail blender,
on and off, while going Pouf!
to me. She winked and smiled.
I thought I knew what she
was up to: Splits! For me!
Wrong. Her husband kind of said:
I'll supply you with a fine
distinction: you served once
in her kitchen. Wow.
I am always boss in her bed,
so shove off, Professor:
thou art too coorse to love.
You mind my grocery store.

MOCK TRANSLATION FROM THE GREEK

Both Erato the Muse of Lyric Poetry and Mime
and Apollo the God of Poetry and Music
are said to be with us, in us, above us, and behind us,
and are often figured to be with a lyre, one
singing and playing with it, and the other
having it at her feet and waiting for action.
If you try to beat him in an arts contest, he'll
skin you alive, the way he did Marsyas, that satyr
who was arrogant enough to challenge him once,
so you have to say, "God, let me have second prize
for my work, after you." Then he might nod,
if you're lucky, he might not even notice you,
if you're lucky, and if you do not listen to HER
when she comes up and talks in your ear,
whether kissingly or bitingly or just breathing something,
and if you don't listen and remember everything she says
or what you think she says, and get it all down,
anytime, anywhere, no matter what else is going on,
oh she will go away, either sadly, or amused, or furious,
or else with no human feelings at all, and leave you
with a mute in your mouth and a bug in your ear,
so you won't be able to hear her saying as she goes away,
        "You know
you stink. What you smell is your own upper lip.
It has to go. Take your last human breath of it, animal.
I'm telling your god Apollo to come down after you."

ON A MYTH.
ON A CONVENTIONAL WISDOM

Who has more fun in bed, men or women,
Zeus asked Tiresias, who had been both,
and when Tiresias answered, Women, of course,
Zeus got so mad he blinded him, he broke his bones,
he sent him back down to earth as a Theban seer.
and you know what happened to Thebes: Pfft!

It was a classic masculine response: We men
have less fun than women in bed, we can't
have children, we can't even have the pleasure
of suckling them, so we go around with empty looks
on our faces looking for excitement, ecstasy, revenge,
we blind people, we break their bones, we destroy Thebes.

This is the classic masculine response, this
is the conventional wisdom, this, we hope, is the myth.

GARGOYLE'S SONG FOR THE WARMING TREND

I am a sewer
useless to myself.
The water of this life
flows in and out of me
the wrong way. No drinks,
while I cry thirst,
no gutter jokes! I puke with it.
I'm all mouth.
Please be my house.
I'll vent your pipes and drains
and sing and roar for you
through the coming rains.

ON A FALLEN STATUE FORBIDDEN TO THE WOMEN AT POMPEII

I was the only man in the world
because I had no tits,
a permanent hard-on and
a prick as big as I was, so I
got packed in sculptor's clay,
holocaust alive in bronze,
and set up in a garden in Pompeii
with a tube run up one leg
and out my cock so I
could come forever to
all comers and flowers
with the fertilizing waters of Vesuvius
as an image of the god, Priapus.

PERVERSE EXPLANATION FOR MUTILATED STATUARY

Her hair was made of poisonous snakes
and her mouth was an open scream,
so when they put their pricks in it
they had the feeling of having come
into nothing at all but a scream,
and the feeling of having been stung
all over. Then, as her teeth closed,
and they opened their eyes to stare,
they turned dead white and froze.

How else did they get there,
set up around Medusa's crypt,
those white statues of sound
young men with the missing pricks,
or with fig leaves over the wound?

ON A SUMMER GODDESS WHO SHOULD BE NAMELESS

There are two things you have
to worry about about her.
She opens up for you
and she closes up on you,
but you shouldn't worry
too much about it because
this is the way she is
and this is the way you are:
You just shouldn't mention her name.
She loves you in her own way
and you love her in your own way
but you should never call her an ox.
If you call a woman an ox you're dead,
so what do you say about a goddess?
She might keep you alive, and in her own hell,
so you have to sweet-talk her to death, your own,
and call her by all sorts of names
like ox-eye daisy, dog-dayes-eye,
gold flower, white flower, clear flower,
Chrysanthemum leucanthemum or *Bellis perennis!,*
anything to avoid it, the name
of the ox-eyed goddess, the one
whose name begins with an H,

has two letters, E and R, and ends in an A,
you know the one I mean,
the one who comes on Midsummer Night
protected by and running that dog,
Sirius, to oversee the crisis
of opening and closing time:
that's when the flowers start
to bloom themselves to death
so that their seeds can blow away
and start up someplace else,
so watch it: do right by her
and her daisies. Beware the dog:
He's called Rusty or Red Dog
or else Blackie or Black Dog because:
If he looks down at you
out of one of his red eyes
if she happens to ask him to
as they swing by overhead,
you and yours and your whole countryside
will be wholly burnt up to black ashes.

NIGHT SCENE BEFORE COMBAT

There are trucks going down our street tonight
in convoy. The window rattles. There are lights
going on and off in the sky
beyond the suburbs, accompanied
by noises that sound like thunder.
I should be with them but
I try to get some sleep
with you. Did you know
that Metaphor means Truck
in Modern Greek? Truck. Carryall.
It figures. As William Blake said,
Eternity is in love with us
creations of time, and you *know*
about love, not just the weapons and battles,
but the problems of supply, logistics,
of getting the material to the front,
to the precise point of fire, in trucks,
at that point of place, at this point in time,
when the lights are flashing on and off
and what might sound like thunder is
not thunder, not thunder at all.
I should go downstairs and join
my outfit, I should get back
to the truck I left idling

by the curb, but I turn to you
for one last time in sleep, love,
before I put my uniform back on,
check my piece, and say So long.

NOTES ABOUT THE AUTHOR

ALAN DUGAN was born in Brooklyn, New York, on February 12, 1923. He went to Queens College, Flushing, New York, for a while, spent World War II in the U.S. Army Air Force, and, afterward, graduated from Mexico City College. He holds a Pulitzer Prize, a National Book Award, and a Prix de Rome. In 1982 he received the Shelley Memorial Award from the Poetry Society of America, and in 1985, an Award in Literature from the American Academy and Institute of Arts and Letters. He is married to the artist Judith Shahn. He has taught at Connecticut College, Sarah Lawrence College, the University of Colorado at Boulder, and other institutions. At present he is a member of the Writing Committee at the Fine Arts Work Center in Provincetown, Massachusetts.